D1015041

ancient romans

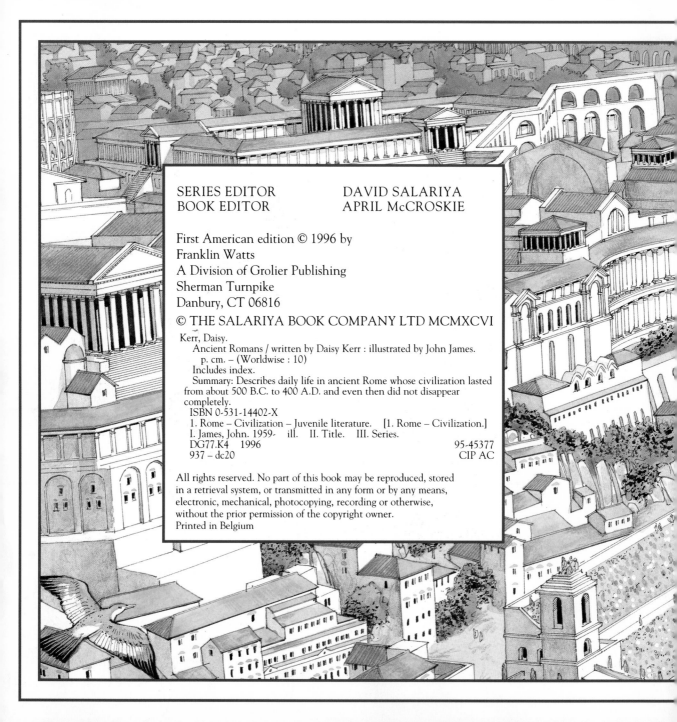

SERIES EDITOR   DAVID SALARIYA
BOOK EDITOR   APRIL McCROSKIE

First American edition © 1996 by
Franklin Watts
A Division of Grolier Publishing
Sherman Turnpike
Danbury, CT 06816
© THE SALARIYA BOOK COMPANY LTD MCMXCVI
Kerr, Daisy.
    Ancient Romans / written by Daisy Kerr : illustrated by John James.
      p. cm. – (Worldwise : 10)
    Includes index.
    Summary: Describes daily life in ancient Rome whose civilization lasted
from about 500 B.C. to 400 A.D. and even then did not disappear
completely.
    ISBN 0-531-14402-X
    1. Rome – Civilization – Juvenile literature.   [1. Rome – Civilization.]
I. James, John. 1959-   ill.   II. Title.   III. Series.
DG77.K4   1996   95-45377
937 – dc20   CIP AC

ancient
romans

Written by
DAISY KERR
Illustrated by
JOHN JAMES

Series Created & Designed by
DAVID SALARIYA

FRANKLIN WATTS
A Division of Grolier Publishing
New York•London•Hong Kong•
Sydney•Danbury, Connecticut

CONTENTS

The Romans lived

in Italy, about 2,000 years ago. At first, they were farmers. They grew rich and powerful. Then they built a fine big city, called Rome. Soon they ruled the mightiest empire the world had ever seen.

Roman civilization lasted for hundreds of years, from around 500 BC to AD 400. Even then, it did not disappear completely. Builders still used Roman designs. Engineers still relied on Roman technology. And we still use many Roman words today.

Rich families were called "patricians." They owned land in the country, and the men also had jobs as government officials.

Roman citizens

believed their city was the best run in the world. It had good laws, fine buildings, fresh water, drains that worked, cheap entertainments, and free food for the poor. At first, Rome was ruled by kings. Then, in 509 BC, it became a republic. It was ruled by officials chosen by the citizens, who voted every year. After 27 BC, Rome was ruled by emperors. Some emperors were wise and fair; others were very bad.

Middle-class families were called "equites." They ran big businesses and owned buildings in the city of Rome.

Ordinary people were called "plebeians." They worked in shops, taverns, and the market. Others were craftworkers.

Slaves

There were millions of slaves in Roman lands. They did the hardest, dirtiest work. They were owned by their master or mistress.

When Rome was a republic, the government was led by two officials called "consuls."

The consuls shared power. New consuls were chosen every year.

The consuls discussed their plans with the senate – a group of past officials who offered wise advice. Members of the senate were called senators. Sometimes the consuls and the senators disagreed.

Quaestor

Praetor

Aedile

Senator

Consul

Senators

Censor

OTHER GOVERNMENT OFFICIALS
Censors kept lists of landowners and sent citizens to join the army.
Aediles looked after public buildings and water supplies.
Praetors and **quaestors** were judges. They tried criminals in the law courts.

The Forum was a large, open-air market in the center of Rome. It was surrounded by shops, offices, and government buildings. The law courts and public meeting rooms were nearby.

Emperors built huge palaces in the center of Rome so everyone could see how powerful they were. They also needed space to store their jewels, sculptures, and other works of art.

Emperor Nero (who ruled AD 54-68) created a park close to his palace. It had water fountains, rare plants, and a zoo.

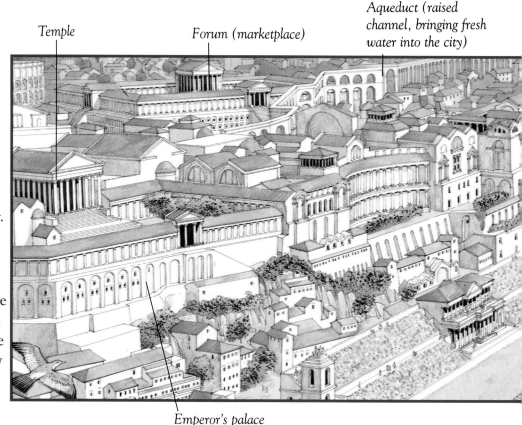

Temple

Forum (marketplace)

Aqueduct (raised channel, bringing fresh water into the city)

Emperor's palace

Rome was a very big city, full of fine buildings. Almost a million people lived there in 50 BC. Some residents were born in Rome, but many others traveled there from the country in search of work.

Circus Maximus
(vast sports arena, where
chariot races were held)

Monuments to
famous sportsmen

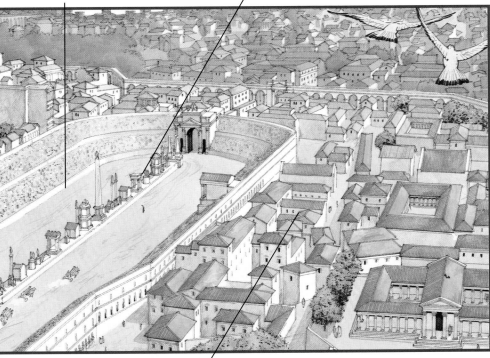

This sculpture shows
the wolf in the legend
of Romulus and
Remus. Legend says
these twin baby boys
were rescued by the
wolf as they floated
down a river. Later in
753 BC, Romulus
built Rome on the site
of the wolf's home.

Rome probably
originated around
800 BC as a group
of little villages,
built on seven
neighboring hills.
The villages grew
larger and joined
to become one
big city.

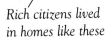

Rich citizens lived
in homes like these

Rome was the center of government, law, and
trade. Well-made roads led to the rest of Italy
and the world beyond, bringing merchants,
travelers, and messengers into the city.
The citizens boasted, "All roads lead to Rome."

Roman towns were noisy, dirty, and crowded. Rich people had big homes, with private gardens and high walls shutting them off from the busy streets. But ordinary people lived in small houses or big blocks of apartments. So they liked to spend time outside, wandering round the shops or chatting with friends.

At night, watchmen patroled the streets, looking out for burglars.

Big blocks of apartments were called "insulae." There were shops at street level and small attics under the roof. The best rooms were on the first floor.

Smallest apartments

Roman streets were paved with stone. There might be an open drain along one side, full of garbage and smelly water. There were public bathrooms and water fountains on many street corners.

Best apartments

Street-level shops

Chariot races often ended in disaster. Chariots crashed into each other as they followed the curve of the track.

Theater tickets were decorated with pictures of the masks Roman actors wore on stage. The masks could be funny or sad.

The Colosseum in Rome, (built AD 80) had 50,000 seats. Turn the page to see what happened there.

Roman audiences enjoyed plays, music, and dancing. But the biggest crowds went to watch chariot races or to see gladiators kill one another and slaughter wild beasts. The animals were tormented until they were ready to attack. Gladiators were often prisoners or slaves, forced to fight until they died. Each time they raced, charioteers and horses risked being killed.

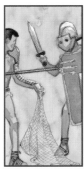

"Reticulares" were armed with nets and tridents (huge forks).

The emperor decided on the life of a defeated gladiator.

A few successful gladiators became rich and famous.

Brave gladiators might be given fine weapons and armor.

"Vilites" were gladiators who threw spears at each other.

Sometimes teams of gladiators fought big battles.

"Bestarii" fought wild animals — snakes, lions, and bears.

Girls from ordinary families were taught how to cook and keep house by their mothers. Rich girls had their own slaves.

Boys from ordinary families were taught craft skills by their fathers.

Grinding grain

Romans worked hard to earn a living. There were over 150 trades, from brewers and corn dealers to wine merchants, tailors, pharmacists, cake bakers, weavers, fish sellers, boot menders, wagon drivers, florists, and goldsmiths. There were thousands of small businesses too, like local taverns and barber shops. Ordinary citizens taught their children the skills they would need in adult life as traders or craftworkers.

Boys from farming families were taught how to grow crops, grind corn, press olives, and make wine.

Skilled craftworkers, like this potter, could earn a good wage.

Clever young slaves were trained to read and write and to keep accounts.

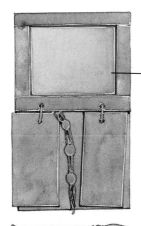

Wax tablets were used for making notes. Words and figures were scratched into the wax using a special metal pen called a stylus, or a pointed stick.

Boy with tutor

Boys from wealthy families went to secondary school when they were twelve. They learned Roman history and studied poems by famous Greek and Roman writers.

Messages written on wax tablets could be rubbed out by melting the wax. The tablets were then ready to use again.

Roman boys were taught to keep fit. Schoolteachers said they should aim to have "a healthy mind in a healthy body."

Boys who wanted a career in the government had to learn how to make speeches in front of large numbers of people.

Boys from wealthy families went to school when they were seven years old. They learned to read and write and do math.

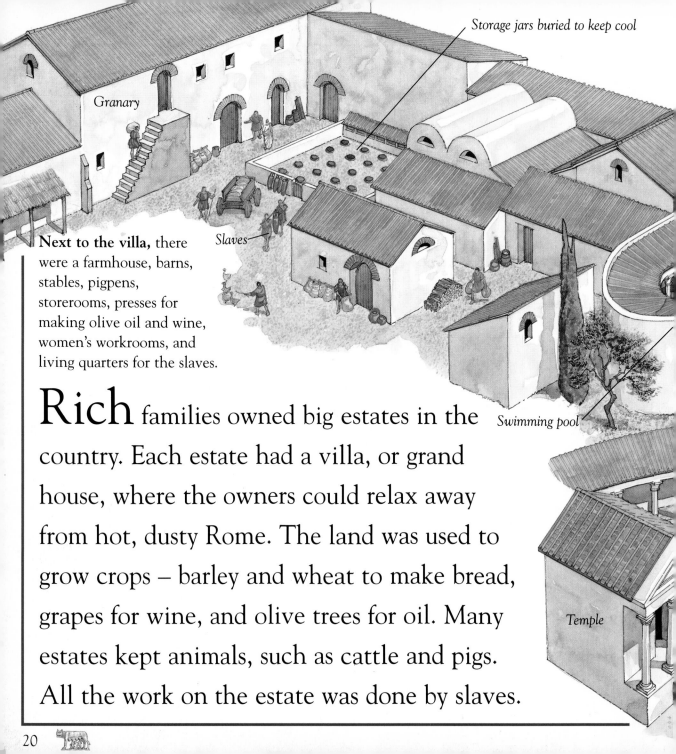

Storage jars buried to keep cool

Granary

Next to the villa, there were a farmhouse, barns, stables, pigpens, storerooms, presses for making olive oil and wine, women's workrooms, and living quarters for the slaves.

Slaves

Swimming pool

Temple

Rich families owned big estates in the country. Each estate had a villa, or grand house, where the owners could relax away from hot, dusty Rome. The land was used to grow crops – barley and wheat to make bread, grapes for wine, and olive trees for oil. Many estates kept animals, such as cattle and pigs. All the work on the estate was done by slaves.

Cool,
shady arcade

Courtyard
garden

Colonnade
(covered walkway)

Entrance
porch to
villa

Garden

Rich Romans liked to be clean and well dressed. Men and women wore tunic-style clothes in fine-spun wool. The best cloth was dyed purple or red. By law, slaves had to wear simple clothes. But nobles wore flowing robes. Summer clothes were loose and airy. Extra layers were added in cold weather.

An ordinary Roman man had only simple clothes to put on: underpants, tunic, and sandals. He might add a thick cloak in winter.

Rich men wore togas (circular cloaks) over their tunics. The best togas had bright purple borders. Only senators and judges in the courts were allowed to wear them.

Wig

Makeup

Stola

Toga

Rich women wore elaborate clothes to show off their wealth. Stolas (floor-length robes), makeup, wigs, and jewelry were fashionable.

Rich women also had body-slaves to mix bath oils and perfumes, put makeup on them, and arrange their hair.

Aqueduct

In 312 BC, government leader Appius Claudius completed the first-ever aqueduct, bringing fresh water to Rome from distant hills. By around AD 100, almost 2.5 million gallons of water flowed into Rome every day.

Romans were expert water engineers. They had clean water for drinking and for the huge public baths in Rome. They built drains to take away sewage and dirty water. The first Roman sewers were dug around 550 BC. The tunnels were so big that carts could be driven through them.

Public bathrooms had rows of seats. Several people could use them at once.

By around AD 100, there were about 1,000 bathhouses in Rome. Turn the page to see inside the public baths.

AT THE BATHS

Undress in the changing room.

Do exercises in the open-air courtyard.

Rinse off sweat and relax in the warm pool.

Rub off dirt in the hot steam room.

Jump into the cold plunge pool.

Romans ate "cena" (dinner) in the late afternoon. They had only one cooked meal each day. Breakfast and lunch were just quick snacks. Ordinary people ate plain food like bread and cheese, porridge, olives, onions, garlic, figs, apples, and grapes.
But rich families liked to invite their friends to banquets, cooked by chefs and served to diners in the "triclinium" (dining room).

Wheat was ground into flour, then mixed with oil and water to make bread dough. This was shaped into loaves and cooked in huge ovens. Bakers made fresh bread every day.

Most homes did not have kitchens or ovens. So, for dinner, people bought ready-cooked meals or ate a cheap meal at a local tavern.

Pottery jar built into the shop counter keeps cooked food warm.

Slave

In wealthy homes, well-trained slaves made all kinds of delicious food. They might be beaten if they burned the dinner.

Rich families offered rare dishes, such as roast ostrich, dormouse in honey, or baked flamingo. Diners ate lying down on couches.

Dinner party guests arrived around 4:00.

Roman wine was very strong, so it was always mixed with water.

Wealthy Romans liked delicate dishes and cups made of silver and glass.

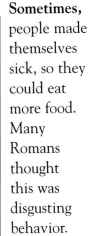

Sometimes, people made themselves sick, so they could eat more food. Many Romans thought this was disgusting behavior.

Guests brought their own napkins, to protect their clothes. Later, they used the same napkins to carry home left-over food.

Roman craftworkers made fine pottery. This bowl is made from "Samian ware."

The Romans believed that seven was the ideal number of people for a dinner party.

27

The Roman Empire
included many
different peoples:
1. Dacian (Romanian)
2. Celt (British
   or French)
3. Numidian
   (North African)
4. Roman Citizen
   (from Italy)
5. Greek
6. Syrian
7. Jew (from Israel)
8. Palmyran
   (Jordanian)

As Rome grew stronger, Roman armies began to conquer more land. First they attacked areas outside Rome, then North Africa, and the Middle East. In 54 BC Roman general Julius Caesar invaded France. In AD 43, the Romans conquered Britain. By AD 100, almost 60 million people were ruled by Rome.

By AD 100, the Roman Empire stretched from Scotland to Egypt and Turkey.

TRAVEL IN THE EMPIRE

Building a
Roman road.

Packhorses
were cheap.

Carts pulled by
pairs of cattle.

Covered horse-
drawn wagons.

Horse and
light carriage.

Litter carried
by slaves.

Carts to
carry mail.

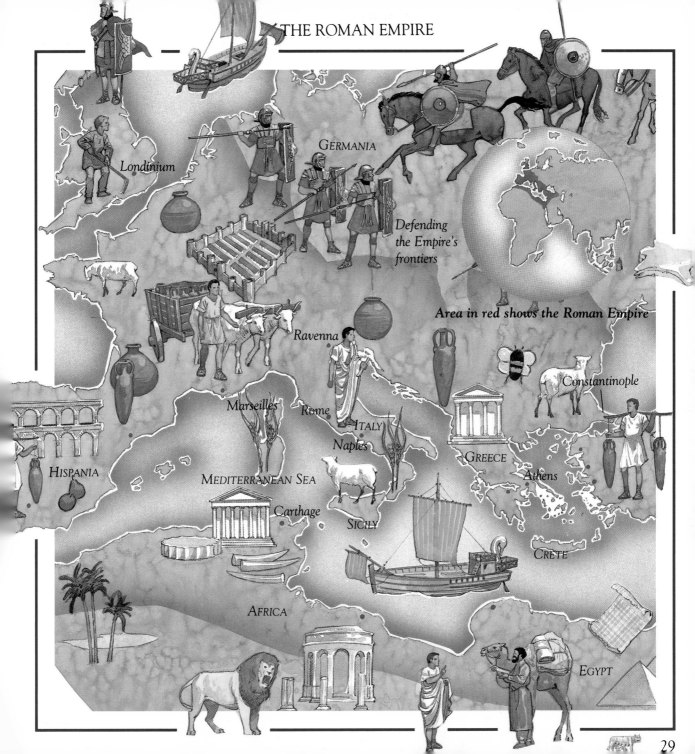

GERMANIA

Londinium

*Defending
the Empire's
frontiers*

Area in red shows the Roman Empire

Ravenna

Marseilles

Rome

ITALY

Naples

Constantinople

HISPANIA

MEDITERRANEAN SEA

GREECE

Athens

Carthage

SICILY

CRETE

AFRICA

EGYPT

29

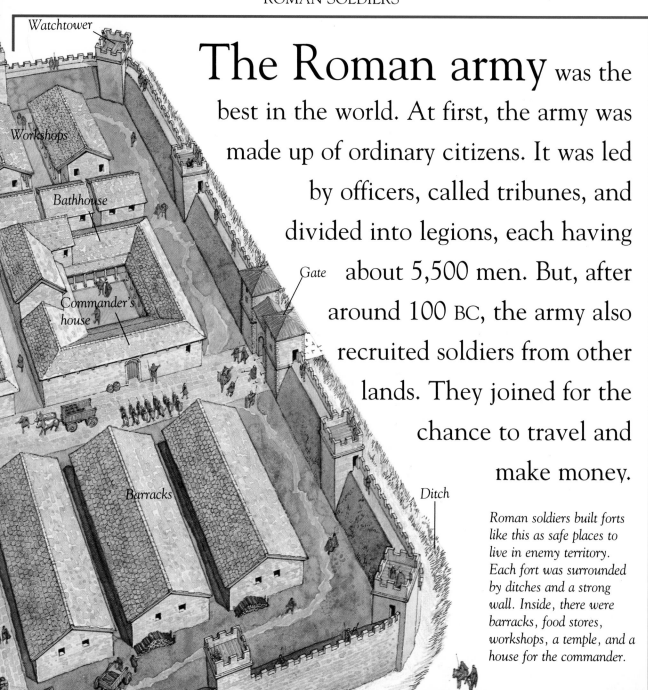

Watchtower

Workshops

Bathhouse

Commander's house

Gate

Barracks

Ditch

The Roman army was the best in the world. At first, the army was made up of ordinary citizens. It was led by officers, called tribunes, and divided into legions, each having about 5,500 men. But, after around 100 BC, the army also recruited soldiers from other lands. They joined for the chance to travel and make money.

Roman soldiers built forts like this as safe places to live in enemy territory. Each fort was surrounded by ditches and a strong wall. Inside, there were barracks, food stores, workshops, a temple, and a house for the commander.

Helmet

Armor made of metal strips

Javelin

Soldiers covered their shoulders, back, and chest with armor made out of metal strips.

Soldiers wore leather sandals – they might have to march up to 50 kilometres a day.

Legionnaires agreed to serve in the army for 25 years. They were paid regular wages.

Short sword

Long sword

Roman soldiers carried a cooking pot and three days' food rations with them. Basic rations were grain and salt, which soldiers cooked over their camp fires to make stew.

Wool tunic

Milestone

Roman roads were built throughout the Empire so that the army could march quickly to trouble spots. Most roads were planned and built by soldiers.

Leather sandals

Road building

Roman soldiers were

well trained. At the start of a battle, archers, sling-shot throwers, and cavalry troops made hit-and-run charges at the enemy, to scare them away. Then the legionnaires advanced on foot, hurling their javelins at the enemy, and stabbing and slashing with their swords. Few nations were strong enough to survive a Roman attack.

Most Roman forts contained a hospital, where injured soldiers could be treated by well-trained doctors.

The Romans invented battering rams, onagers (which hurled stones), and assault towers (for getting to the enemy over the top of walls).

Roman doctors prepared mixtures of herbs and plants to ease the patients' pain during operations. Doctors tried to keep wounds clean, but many patients died from infections after operations or injuries.

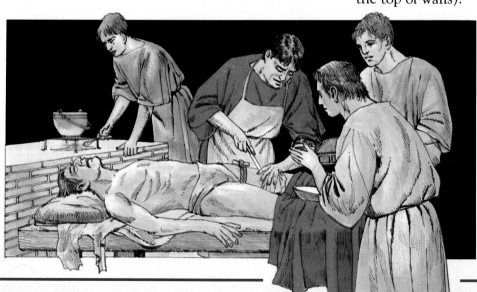

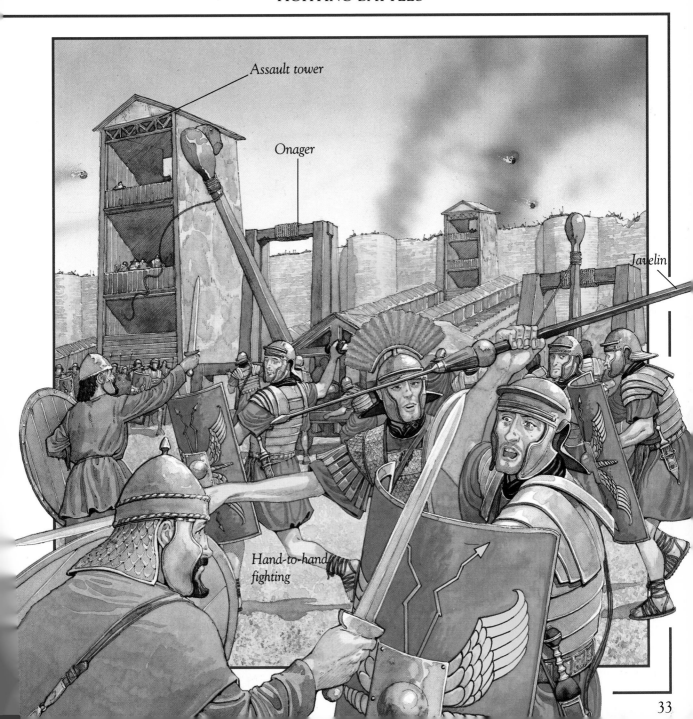

Assault tower

Onager

Javelin

Hand-to-hand
fighting

Romans built temples as homes for their gods and goddesses.

Jupiter

Every day, families said prayers to the "Lares" and "Penates." These were the gods who protected the household. On holy days, they left offerings of food.

Altar

Bull

Priest

Jupiter was king of the gods. He controled thunder and lightning. Neptune was god of the sea. Mars was the god of war and his wife, Venus, was the goddess of love. The gloomy god Pluto ruled the kingdom of the dead.

At festivals, animals might be killed as sacrifices. The Romans believed that sacrifices pleased the gods. Animals being sacrificed were killed at altars in front of the city's biggest temples.

The Romans worshiped many different gods and goddesses. They all had special powers to guide or protect people who prayed to them. Each god had a special temple, close to the Forum (marketplace).

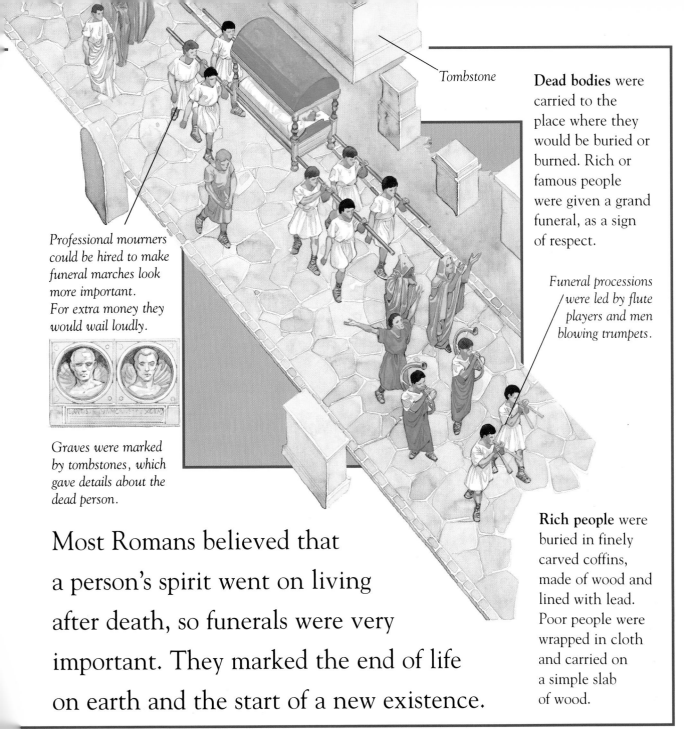

Tombstone

Dead bodies were carried to the place where they would be buried or burned. Rich or famous people were given a grand funeral, as a sign of respect.

Professional mourners could be hired to make funeral marches look more important. For extra money they would wail loudly.

Funeral processions were led by flute players and men blowing trumpets.

Graves were marked by tombstones, which gave details about the dead person.

Most Romans believed that a person's spirit went on living after death, so funerals were very important. They marked the end of life on earth and the start of a new existence.

Rich people were buried in finely carved coffins, made of wood and lined with lead. Poor people were wrapped in cloth and carried on a simple slab of wood.

Statue

Life-size stone statues were made in honor of famous Roman leaders and army commanders.

Coin

Coins often had a portrait of the emperor who was ruling at the time they were made. This tells us how old they are.

Many types of evidence have survived to tell us about life in Roman times. There are ruins of Roman buildings in the city of Rome and in Roman Empire lands. There are paintings and statues, carvings and tombstones, and monuments made to record Roman war victories. Remains have been found at places where the Romans once lived – weapons, pottery, metalwork coins, and glass. And Roman scholars and historians wrote down many descriptions of Roman life, which we can still read today.

Luxury goods, like these jugs, jars, and dishes, were traded throughout the Empire. They can tell us about the artistic tastes and the extravagant life-styles of the rich Romans who used them.

Pompeii was a town near Naples in southern Italy. It was rebuilt after an earthquake in AD 62. But in AD 79, the nearby volcano Vesuvius erupted, burying the town under tons of ash and lava.

Pompeii lay hidden for hundreds of years. In 1784, the King of Naples decided to excavate (dig away) the ash and lava. His workers found the ruined town hidden underneath, like a time capsule.

Dead bodies were covered in ash and lava. This cooled to form a solid block. Inside, the bodies rotted away. Later, plaster was poured into the holes left by the rotted bodies to make "casts."

When Vesuvius erupted, people tried to escape. But most of them were killed by clouds of poisonous gas before they could get away.

Today, tourists from all over the world visit Pompeii to walk around the ruined Roman houses and streets.

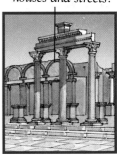

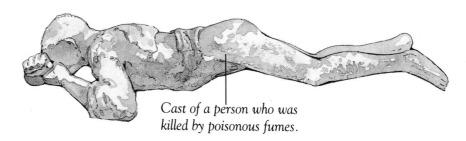

Cast of a person who was killed by poisonous fumes.

USEFUL WORDS

Aediles Junior government officials, in charge of public works.

Aqueduct Raised channel, built to carry water.

Barracks Buildings where soldiers live.

Cena Dinner (eaten in the late afternoon or evening).

Censors Junior government officials in charge of land ownership.

Citizens People who live in a city.

Consuls Leaders of the government in republican Rome.

Emperor Strong ruler, who has total power.

Empire Lands ruled by a foreign power.

Equites Roman citizens who were rich but not noble.

Forum Marketplace.

Gladiators Men who fought and died to entertain Roman crowds.

Lava Hot rock, inside volcanoes.

Litter Covered bed carried by slaves.

Patricians Nobles.

Plebeians Ordinary people.

Praetor Judge in Roman courts.

Questor Junior judge in Roman courts.

Republic Government by elected officials.

Senate Group of past government officials in republican Rome.

Senators Members of the senate.

Slave Person who is owned by someone else.

Toga Circular cloak worn by noble men.

Villa Grand country house.

INDEX